Contents

Meets **Accreditation Standard** for **Child-created Bulletin Boards**

Introduction

This series of monthly activity books is designed to give PreK and Kindergarten teachers a collection of hands-on activities and ideas for each month of the year. The activities are standards-based and reflect the philosophy that children learn best through play. The teacher can use these ideas to enhance the development of language and math skills, and of social/emotional and physical growth of children. The opportunity to promote pre-reading skills is present throughout the series and should be incorporated whenever possible.

Organization and Features

Each book consists of seven units:

Unit 1 provides reproducible pages and information for the month in general.
- a newsletter outline to promote parent communication
- a blank thematic border page
- a list of special days in the month
- calendar ideas to promote math skills
- a blank calendar grid that can also be used as an incentive chart

Units 2–6 include an array of activities for five **theme** topics. Each unit includes:
- teacher information on the theme
- arts and crafts ideas
- a food activity
- poetry, songs, and books
- bulletin board ideas
- center activities correlated to specific learning standards

Implement the activities in a way that best meets the needs of individual children.

Unit 7 focuses on a well-known **children's author**. The unit includes
- a biography of the author
- activities based on a literature selection
- a list of books by the author
- reproducible bookmarks

In addition, each book contains
- reproducible **icons** suitable to use as labels for centers in the classroom. The icons coordinate with the centers in the book. They may also be used with a work assignment chart to aid in assigning children to centers.
- reproducible **student awards**
- **calendar day pattern** with suggested activities

Research Base

Howard Gardner's theory of multiple intelligences, or learning styles, validates teaching thematically and using a variety of approaches to help children learn. Providing a variety of experiences will assure that each child has an opportunity to learn in a comfortable way.

Following are the learning styles identified by Howard Gardner.
- **Verbal/Linguistic** learners need opportunities to read, listen, write, learn new words, and to tell stories.
- **Musical** learners enjoy music activities.
- **Logical/Mathematical** learners need opportunities to problem solve, count, measure, and do patterning activities.
- **Visual/Spatial** learners need opportunities to paint, draw, sculpt, and create art works.
- **Interpersonal** learners benefit from group discussions and group projects.
- **Intrapersonal** learners learn best in solitary activities, such as reading, writing in journals, and reflecting on information.
- **Naturalist** learners need opportunities to observe weather and nature and to take care of animals and plants.
- **Existential** learners can be fostered in the early years by asking children to think and respond, by discussions, and journal writing.

Gardner, H. (1994). *Frames of mind.* New York: Basic Books.

January News

Teacher: _____ Date: _____

Headline News

Coming Up

Happy Birthday to

Special Thanks to

Help Wanted

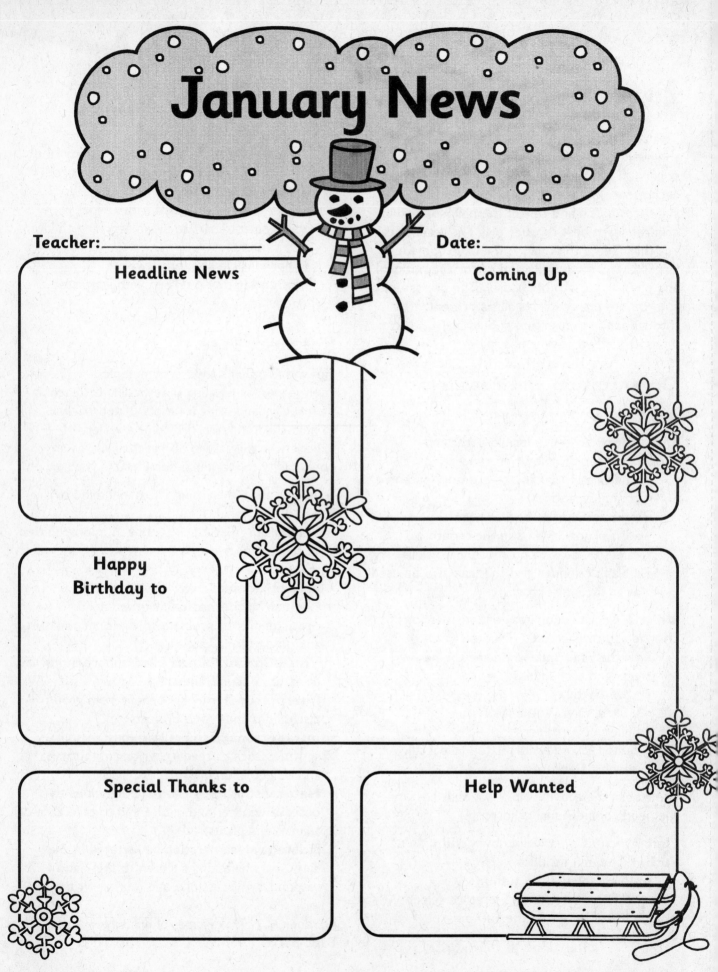

Three Cheers for January PreK–K, SV 9312-2

January

Special Days in January

National Hobby Month   Discuss with children hobbies that they might enjoy doing such as playing a sport, taking lessons to learn something new, or starting a collection.

National Candy Month   Have children sample three different types of candy and record their favorite kind on a graph.

1 New Year's Day   Have children celebrate with activities from the New Year's Unit that begins on page 10.

 4 Louis Braille's Birthday   Have children cover their eyes with a blindfold and hold an object in their hands. Challenge them to name the object without using their eyes.

5 National Bird Day   Take a walk around the school grounds and count how many birds the children see on the walk.

8 Elvis Presley's Birthday   Show a picture of Elvis and play a song by Elvis. Let children dance to the music.

 15 Martin Luther King, Jr.'s Birthday   Read *A Picture Book of Martin Luther King, Jr.* by David A. Adler (Holiday House). Discuss with children the feelings that they have when someone says unkind words to them.

18 A. A. Milne's Birthday   Display a picture of Winnie the Pooh. Have children tell what they know about the character. Read a story about Winnie the Pooh.

 19 Popcorn Day   Have children sit around the edge of a clean sheet. Pop popcorn using an air popper and let children watch the popcorn fly. Eat for a snack.

 21 National Hugging Day   Give each child a special hug at the beginning and at the end of the day.

28 Ernie's Birthday   Read a book about Bert and Ernie. Have children tell what they like about Ernie.

31 Backwards Day   Read *Backwards Day (Let's Have A Party, No. 8)* by Laura E. Williams (Avon). Have children wear their clothes backwards and reverse the order of the day's schedule.

Three Cheers for January PreK–K, SV 9312-2

January

Sunday	Monday	Tuesday	Wednesday	Thursday	Friday	Saturday

Unit 1, Teacher Resources: January Calendar

Three Cheers for January PreK–K, SV 9312-2

Calendar Activities for January

Classroom Calendar Setup

The use of the calendar in the classroom can provide children with daily practice on learning days, weeks, months, and years. As you plan the setup for your classroom, include enough space on the wall to staple a calendar grid labeled with the days of the week. Leave space above the grid for the name of the month and the year. Next to the calendar, staple twelve cards labeled with the months of the year and the number of days in each month. (Use the calendar day pattern on page 96.) Leave these items on the wall all year. At the beginning of each month, start with the blank calendar grid. Do not staple anything on the grid that refers to the new month. Leave the days of the week and the year in place.

Introducing the Month of January

Before children arrive, gather all of the items that will go on the calendar for January. You may want to include the name of the month, number cards, name cards to indicate birthdays during the month, and picture cards that tell about special holidays or school events during the month. You may also wish to wrap a small treat such as sugarless gum which can be taped on the day of each child's birthday. Add a special pointer that can be used each day while doing calendar activities. See page 9 for directions on how to make a pointer. Place these items in a picnic basket. Select a puppet that can remain in the basket and come out only to bring items for each new month. A dog puppet works well because of the large mouth which makes it easier to grasp each item.

Place the picnic basket in front of the class. Pull out the puppet and introduce it to children if it is the first time they have seen it or ask them if they remember why the puppet is here. If this is the first time they have seen it, explain that the puppet will visit on the first day of each month to bring the new calendar items. Then have the puppet pull out the name of the month. According to the abilities of children, have them name the first letter in the name of the month, count the letters or find the vowels. Staple the name of the month above the calendar. Have the puppet pull out the new pointer for the teacher or the daily helper to use each day during calendar time.

Next, pull out the number cards for January. You may use plain number cards, or you may want to use seasonal die-cut shapes. By using two or three die-cut shapes, you can incorporate building patterns as part of your daily calendar routine. See page 9 for pattern ideas. Place the number one card or die-cut under the day of the week on which January begins. Locate January on the month cards that are stapled next to your calendar. Have children tell how many days this month will have and then count that many spaces on the calendar to indicate the end of the month. You may wish to place a small stop sign as a visual reminder of the end of the month. Save the remaining number card or die-cut shapes and add one each day.

If there are any birthdays during January, have the puppet pull out of the basket the cards that have a birthday symbol with the child's name and birth date written on it. Count from the number 1 to find where to staple this as a visual reminder of each child's birthday. If you have included a wrapped treat for each child, tape it on the calendar on the correct day.

Finally, have the puppet bring out cards that have pictures of holidays or special happenings, such as field trips, picture day, or story time in the library. Staple the picture cards on the correct day on the calendar grid. You can use these to practice various counting skills such as counting how many days until a field trip, a birthday, or a holiday. When the basket is empty, say goodbye to the puppet and return it to the picnic basket. Put the basket away until the next month. Children will look forward to the beginning of each month in order to see what items the puppet will bring for the class calendar.

Making a Glove Pointer

Include a glove pointer in the calendar basket for this month. To make a pointer, you will need one knitted glove (any color), some narrow ribbon, a small amount of polyester fiberfill, and a medium-sized dowel rod that is 18" long. Stuff the glove with the fiberfill until it takes the shape of a hand. Bend the thumb and fingers down, leaving the pointer finger extended, and stitch in place. Cover the end of the dowel rod with hot glue and insert it into the glove. Secure the glove to the rod by tying the ribbon around the wrist.

Developing a Pattern

Practice patterning by writing the numbers 1–31 on three die-cut shapes, such as a snowman, a mitten, and a snowman's hat. Place the shapes in order using an ABBCABBC pattern. As the children add a shape for each day of the month, they will begin to see the pattern develop. Challenge them to predict the shape for specific days. For example, what will the shape be on the last Thursday of the month or on a child's birthday?

New Year's Celebrations

 The Babylonians were the first to celebrate the New Year about 4,000 years ago. Their new year began with the first new moon after the first day of spring, and the celebration lasted eleven days.

 Around the time of Julius Caesar, the Romans tried to synchronize the calendar with the sun. They declared January 1 to be the beginning of the New Year.

 The making of New Year's resolutions dates back to the early Babylonians, and the tradition of using a baby to signify the New Year was begun in Greece around 600 B.C.

 Traditional New Year's foods are thought to bring good luck in the coming year.

 The Jewish New Year is called *Rosh Hashanah*. Special services are held in the synagogue during this holy time.

 The date of the Muslim New Year is based on the movement of the moon and is celebrated in March. People jump over fire on the last Tuesday of the year to symbolize purification in this non-religious celebration.

 Chinese New Year is celebrated sometime between January 17 and February 19. Their traditions include a New Year's Eve dinner, giving Hongbao or red packets with money to the children, dragon and lion dancing, and a Lantern Festival to mark the end of New Year's celebrations.

New Year's Time Capsule

Materials

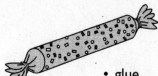

- activity master on page 19
- empty paper towel rolls
- colored tissue paper
- tape
- rubber bands
- sequins, confetti, glitter
- glue
- markers
- photo of each child

Directions

Teacher Preparation: Provide a copy of the activity master for each child. Cut squares of tissue paper that are 6" wider than paper towel rolls.

1. Dictate answers to questions on the activity master.

2. Fold the completed activity master and place it inside the paper tube.

3. Insert a current photo of the child in the tube.

4. Cover the tube with a tissue paper square and tape.

5. Twist the ends of the tissue paper and secure with rubber bands.

6. Decorate the tube with sequins, confetti, or glitter.

7. Write the current year on the side of the tube.

Note: Tell children that time capsules can be saved for any period of time. Encourage them to save their time capsule and open it when they are 10 years old.

Accordion Chinese Dragon

Materials

- patterns on page 20
- 9" x 12" yellow construction paper
- wiggly eyes
- 9" x 12" red construction paper
- sequins or glitter
- feathers
- straws
- markers
- scissors
- glue, tape

Directions

Teacher Preparation: Duplicate the dragon head and tail pattern on yellow construction paper. Provide a copy for each child. Cut red construction paper in half lengthwise.

1. Cut out the head and tail of the dragon.

2. Glue a wiggly eye on both sides of the head.

3. Decorate the head and tail with markers, sequins, glitter, and feathers.

4. Accordion fold a half sheet of red construction paper.

5. Glue one end of the red paper to the head and other end to the tail to form the body of the dragon.

6. Tape one straw to the head and one straw to the tail to use as handles.

7. You can now make your dragon dance for Chinese New Year.

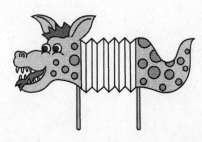

Edible New Year's Hat

You will need

- pointed ice cream cones
- frosting
- shredded carrots
- cake sprinkles
- gumdrops
- paper plates
- jumbo craft sticks

Directions

1. Spread frosting to cover the ice cream cone.
2. Sprinkle shredded carrots over the cone.
3. Cover the cone with cake sprinkles.
4. Put a gumdrop on the point of the cone.
5. Celebrate by eating this New Year's hat!

Tip: Add a few drops of food coloring to the frosting to give it a festive look.

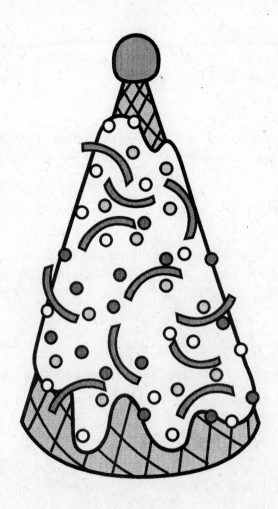

Three Cheers for January PreK–K, SV 9312-2

♫ We Wish You A Happy New Year

(Sing to the tune of "We Wish You A Merry Christmas.")

We wish you a Happy New Year.

We wish you a Happy New Year.

We wish you a Happy New Year.

With lots of good luck!

Gung Hay Fat Choy.

Gung Hay Fat Choy.

Gung Hay Fat Choy.

We sing in Chinese.

Feliz Año Nuevo.

Feliz Año Nuevo.

Feliz Año Nuevo.

We sing in Spanish.

Bringing in the New Year with Books

Amanda Dade's New Year Parade
by Harriet Ziefert (Puffin)

Dragon Dance
by Joan Holub (Puffin)

Happy, Happy Chinese New Year
by Demi Hitz (Random House Children's Books)

Happy New Year, Pooh!
by Robin Cuddy (Disney Press)

New Year's Day
by David F. Marx (Children's Press)

Sammy Spider's First Rosh Hashanah
by Sylvia A. Rouss (Kar-Ben Publishing)

The Dancing Dragon
by Marcia K. Vaughn (Mondo Publishing)

Gung Hay Fat Choy

Materials

- pattern on page 21
- blue craft paper
- 6" x 9" yellow construction paper
- 2" red construction paper triangles
- 2" red tissue paper squares
- sequins or confetti
- scissors
- markers
- glue
- stapler

Directions

Teacher Preparation: Cover the bulletin board with blue craft paper. Duplicate the pattern. Color the head with markers using bright colors and cut it out. Staple the head to the bulletin board.

Find China on the globe and discuss with children some of the traditions of Chinese New Year. Tell children that Gung Hay Fat Choy means Happy New Year in Chinese.

1. Glue red triangles across the top edge of each sheet of construction paper.

2. Glue red tissue paper squares on the construction paper for the scales of the dragon.

3. Add sequins and confetti to decorate.

4. Staple the yellow decorated rectangles on the bulletin board to form a long, winding body for the dragon.

5. Add a yellow tail to the end of the dragon's body.

Three Cheers for January PreK–K, SV 9312-2

New Year's Celebrations Centers

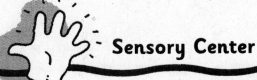

Sensory Center

Social Studies Standard
Identifies customs associated with holidays

It's Party Time

Materials

- large plastic tub
- plastic champagne glasses
- spoons
- holes from paper punch
- plastic beads, bracelets, or rings
- confetti

Teacher Preparation: Fill the plastic tub with confetti and paper punch holes. Add plastic jewelry, champagne glasses, and spoons.

Discuss with children ways that people celebrate the beginning of a new year. Have children use the spoons to fill the glasses with confetti and to also find the party jewelry.

Language Center

Language Arts Standard
Matches words with opposite meanings

Ring Out the Old and Bring In the New

Materials

- picture cards on pages 22 and 23
- library pocket
- glue
- scissors
- file folder
- construction paper
- crayons or markers

Teacher Preparation: Duplicate the picture cards. Color and cut out the cards. Arrange and glue the cards on page 22 on the file folder. Glue the cards on page 23 on construction paper and cut them out. Glue a library pocket to the back of the file folder and use it to store the cards.

Discuss the ending of a year and the beginning of a new year with children. Tell them that the opposite of *old* is *new*. Have children match the picture cards with their opposites on the file folder.

Three Cheers for January PreK–K, SV 9312-2

New Year's Celebrations Centers

Art Center

Chinese Wall Hangings

Materials

- 6" x 12" thin white paper
- white glue
- thin paintbrush
- water
- small paper cups
- black tempera paint
- colored chalk

Teacher Preparation: Squeeze white glue into a paper cup and add a small dot of black paint. Mix using a paintbrush. Hang paper on the art easel. Fill a clean paper cup half full with water.

Display a Chinese wall hanging that families use to decorate their homes. If one is not available, follow the directions below to make one. Be sure to include several Chinese characters for children to see. Explain to them that Chinese characters are not like the English alphabet and that Chinese writing is written from top to bottom not from left to right.

Have children draw thin black lines to make Chinese-like characters on one side of the paper going from top to bottom. Have children dip colored chalk in the water and draw a picture on the blank side of paper beside the letters.

Dramatic Play Center

Ring in the New Year

Materials

- party hats
- old party dresses and shoes
- plastic party glasses
- toy clock
- noisemakers
- old jackets and bow ties
- curly party streamers

Discuss the tradition of welcoming the New Year by making noise and singing when the clock strikes midnight. Show children where the hands on the clock are at midnight. Encourage them to role-play attending a New Year's Eve party.

New Year's Celebrations Centers

Math Center

Math Standard
Knows the values of a penny, nickel, and dime

How Much Is in the Red Packets?

Materials

- pattern on page 24
- black marker
- plastic bowl
- red construction paper
- pennies, nickels, dimes
- glue
- scissors

Teacher Preparation: Duplicate eight copies of the pattern on red construction paper. Assemble the packets and laminate. Write on each packet an amount of money such as 2¢, 5¢, or 7¢. Place coins that are familiar to children in a plastic bowl. For younger children, use only pennies.

Discuss the cents symbol with children. Explain to them that giving Hongbao, or red packets, is a tradition during Chinese New Year. A red packet is a red envelope with money in it that symbolizes good luck. Red packets are handed out to children by family members.

Have children count the amount of money indicated on each packet and place the money in the corresponding packet.

Writing Center

Social Studies Standard
Recognizes the importance of different cultures

New Year's Greetings

Materials

- chart paper
- black markers
- red and white construction paper

Teacher Preparation: Write the words *Gung Hay Fat Choy* on chart paper and display it in the writing center.

Explain to children that *Gung Hay Fat Choy* means Happy New Year in Chinese. Have them use the red and white paper to make greeting cards. Tell children to fold the paper in half and use a black marker to copy the words on the front of the card. Then have children write the name of the person the card is for, such as "Mom" or "Dad."

New Year's Celebrations Centers

Game Center

Math Standard
Counts backwards from 10 to 1

New Year's Countdown

Materials

- large sections of bubble wrap
- masking tape

Teacher Preparation: Tape a large section of bubble wrap to the floor.

Discuss with children the tradition of counting down the last ten seconds until midnight on New Year's Eve. Explain that many people pop firecrackers at the stroke of midnight. Have children work with a partner. Have one child stand on the bubble wrap while the other one counts backwards from 10 to 1. Have the child stomp on the bubble wrap to make the sound of firecrackers when the count gets to one. Have children switch partners and repeat the activity.

Music Center

Social Studies Standard
Identifies customs associated with holidays

Dancing Dragons

Materials

- pattern on page 21
- sentence strips
- glue
- construction paper
- crepe paper streamers
- tape
- markers
- stapler

Teacher Preparation: Duplicate a copy of the pattern on construction paper for each child. Cut out the eyes of the dragon.

Have children color the dragon mask with markers, cut it out, and staple it to the center of a sentence strip. Then help each child wrap the sentence strip around his or her head and staple the ends to fit. Also tape two 3' pieces of crepe paper around the upper part of both of the child's arms. The streamers may hang to the floor.

Play festive music while children pretend to be dancing dragons. When the music stops, the dragons should freeze.

All About Me in 20___

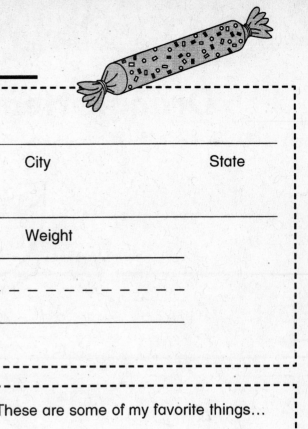

_____

School   Year   City   State

_____

Age   Height   Weight

- -

_____

My Signature

My best friends are _____

_____

_____ .

When I grow up,
I would like to be _____

_____

_____ .

What I like most
about school is _____

_____

_____ .

Pets I have or would
like to have are _____

_____

_____ .

These are some of my favorite things...

_____

Toy

_____

TV Show

_____

Color

_____

Movie

_____

Restaurant

Directions: Use with "New Year's Time Capsule" on page 11. Have children write or dictate their responses. Then have them place their paper in a time capsule.

Three Cheers for January PreK–K, SV 9312-2

Dragon Head and Tail Patterns

Use with "Accordion Chinese Dragon" on page 11.

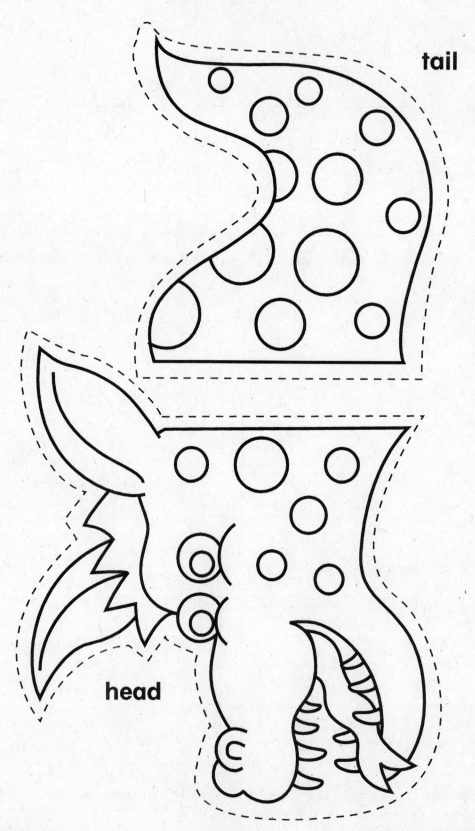

tail

head

Three Cheers for January PreK–K, SV 9312-2

Bulletin Board Pattern

Use with "Gung Hay Fat Choy" on page 14.

head

Three Cheers for January PreK–K, SV 9312-2

Opposites Picture Cards #1

Use with "Ring Out the Old and Bring In the New" on page 15.

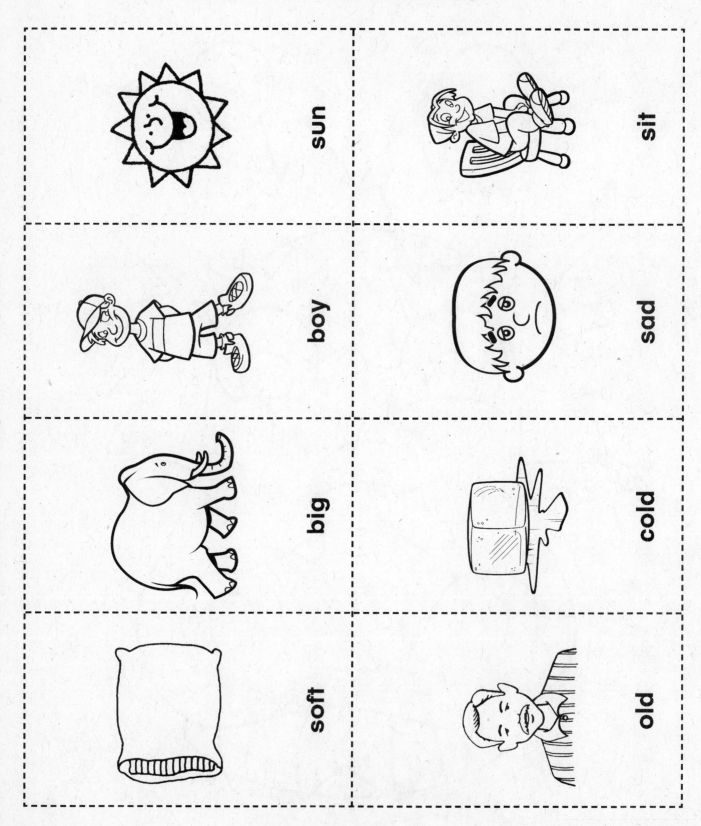

sun

sit

boy

sad

big

cold

soft

old

Three Cheers for January PreK–K, SV 9312-2

Opposites Picture Cards #2

Use with "Ring Out the Old and Bring In the New" on page 15.

moon

stand

girl

happy

little

hot

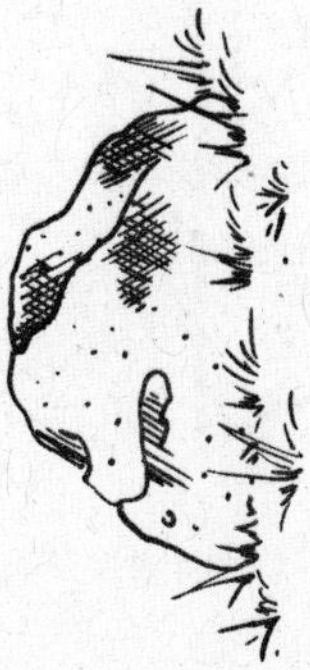

hard

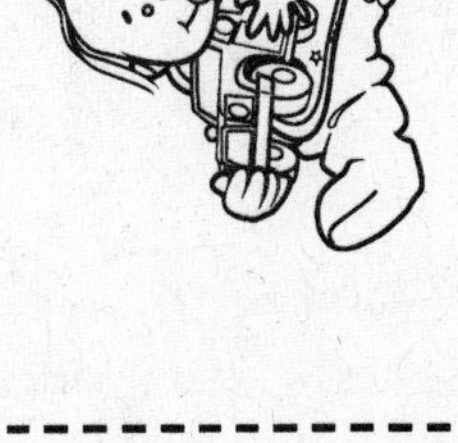

young

Unit 2, New Year's Celebrations: Picture Cards

Three Cheers for January PreK–K, SV 9312-2

Red Packet Pattern

Use with "How Much Is in the Red Packets?" on page 17.

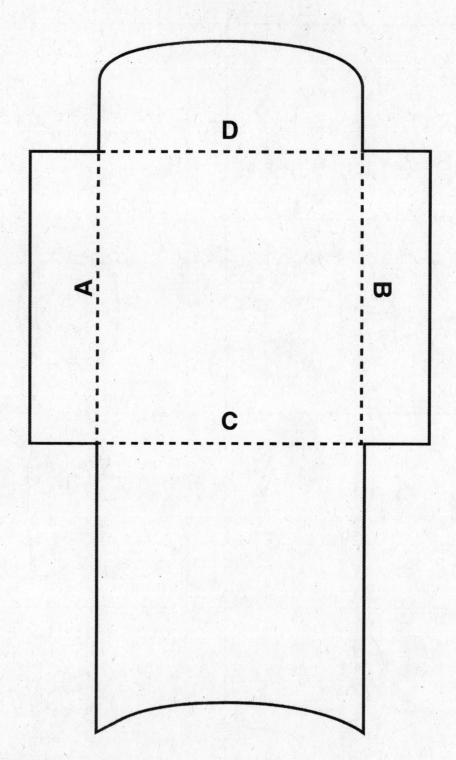

Directions

1. Fold in sides A and B.
2. Fold in side C and glue to sides A and B.
3. Fold side D down for flap.

24

A Fable: The Gingerbread Man

Comparing Versions

 A fable is a story in which most of the characters are animals acting as people in order to teach a lesson or moral.

 Authors often retell or write different versions of popular fables using their own illustrations.

 The Cajun Gingerbread Boy by Berthe Amoss (MTC Press) provides an interesting glimpse into the Louisiana Bayou. The text is written using a gentle Cajun storytelling technique and includes an interesting crocodile.

 Musubi Man: Hawaii's Gingerbread Man by Sandi Takayama (Bess Press, Inc.) provides another spin on the story. A freshly baked musubi man jumps out of an old woman's oven and runs away from his pursuers in this Hawaiian version.

 The Gingerbread Boy by Richard Egielski (Harper Trophy) has the delectable doughboy dashing through the streets of New York City. This tale ends in Central Park after he is chased by a group of hungry New Yorkers.

 Ying Chang Compestine's story of *The Runaway Rice Cake* (Simon and Schuster) conveys an important message about sharing and compassion. On Chinese New Year, the Chang family has only enough rice flour to make one special New Year's rice cake. Of course, the rice cake escapes, but this time the story has a heartwarming ending.

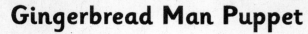

Gingerbread Man Puppet

Materials

- patterns on page 34
- brown construction paper
- jumbo craft stick
- hole punch
- 1-inch brads
- scissors
- glue
- markers

Directions

Teacher Preparation: Duplicate the patterns on brown construction paper for each child.

1. Cut out body, arms, and legs of the gingerbread man.
2. Glue the body to a craft stick.
3. Punch holes where indicated.
4. Attach arms and legs with brads.
5. Draw a face on the gingerbread man.
6. Move the gingerbread man up and down to make him run.

Stuffed Gingerbread Man

Materials

- brown grocery bags
- polyester fiberfill
- pattern on page 35
- scissors
- stapler
- buttons
- black beans
- black marker
- glue

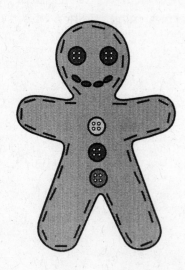

Directions

Teacher Preparation: Duplicate the pattern and cut it out to use as a template. Cut apart each grocery bag and lay it flat. Trace the template on each grocery bag and provide two bags for each child.

1. Cut out the two gingerbread men and put them together.
2. Staple along the edges, leaving the edges around the head open.
3. Stuff the gingerbread man with fiberfill.
4. Staple around the edges of the head.
5. Glue buttons for the eyes and down the front of the gingerbread man.
6. Glue beans for the mouth.

Toasty Gingerbread Men

You will need

- wheat bread
- gingerbread man cookie cutter
- creamy peanut butter or cream cheese
- mini chocolate chips
- red tube frosting
- paper plates
- craft stick or plastic knife

Directions

Teacher Preparation: Toast bread before using if desired.

1. Cut bread into a gingerbread man shape with the cookie cutter.

2. Use the craft stick or knife to cover the gingerbread man with peanut butter or cream cheese.

3. Stick on chocolate chips for the eyes and the buttons.

4. Squeeze a thin line of red frosting for the mouth.

5. Eat before he runs away!

Note: Be aware of children who may have allergies to peanuts.

♫ Gingerbread Man Song

(Sing to the tune of "The Muffin Man.")

Provide children with a gingerbread man cookie. Have them eat the cookie after singing the last line of the song.

Oh, did you see the Gingerbread Man,

The Gingerbread Man,

The Gingerbread Man?

Oh, did you see the Gingerbread Man,

Who ran and ran and ran?

He said, "Catch me if you can,

If you can, if you can."

He said, "Catch me if you can,"

Then ran and ran and ran.

The fox ate up the Gingerbread Man,

The Gingerbread Man, the Gingerbread Man.

The fox ate up the Gingerbread Man,

I can, too. I can, I can.

Great Gingerbread Books

Gingerbread Baby
by Jan Brett (Putnam Publishing Group)

Gingerbread Man
by Eric A. Kimmel (Holiday House)

Gingerbread Man
by Karen Schmidt (Scholastic, Inc.)

Maisy Makes Gingerbread
by Lucy Cousins (Candlewick Press)

Musubi Man: Hawaii's Gingerbread Man
by Sandi Takayama (Bess Press, Inc.)

The Cajun Gingerbread Boy
illustrated by Berthe Amoss (MTC Press)

The Gingerbread Boy
by Richard Egielski (Harper Trophy)

Three Cheers for January PreK–K, SV 9312-2

Gingerbread Cookies

Materials

- pattern on page 35
- sandpaper
- cinnamon sticks
- scissors
- aluminum foil
- one sheet of poster board
- pink or white puff paint
- red rickrack
- glue

Directions

Teacher Preparation: Duplicate the pattern and cut it out to make a template. Trace the template on the back of a sheet of sandpaper and cut it out. Provide a copy for each child. Cover the poster board with foil to look like a cookie sheet.

1. Rub a cinnamon stick across the sandpaper side of a gingerbread man for a wonderful scent.

2. Glue red rickrack on for the mouth.

3. Squeeze dots of puff paint on the gingerbread man for the eyes, nose, and buttons.

Tip: Older children can cut out the gingerbread men if a medium or fine sandpaper is used.

Three Cheers for January PreK–K, SV 9312-2

The Gingerbread Man Centers

Art Center

Science Standard
Understands properties of materials

A "Scent-sational" Gingerbread Man

Materials

- bottle of ground cinnamon
- wooden spoon
- mixing bowl
- toothpicks
- I cup applesauce
- rolling pin
- magnetic tape
- small gingerbread man cookie cutter

Teacher Preparation: Mix the applesauce and cinnamon to form a stiff dough. Provide each child with a 2" ball of dough. Sprinkle cinnamon on the table before rolling the dough to prevent sticking.

Have children use a rolling pin to flatten the ball of dough to about ¼ inch thickness. Then have them cut out a gingerbread man with a cookie cutter. Invite children to use the tip of a toothpick to make eyes, a mouth, and buttons on the gingerbread man.

Allow the children's gingerbread men to air-dry for 72 hours. Or you can bake them at 150°F for 5–6 hours. When they are completely dry, have children press a small piece of magnetic tape to the back of their gingerbread man. Encourage children to take their gingerbread man home, place it on the refrigerator, and enjoy the scent.

Tip: Have children participate in mixing the ingredients. Then invite them to eat applesauce with a sprinkle of cinnamon on top for a snack.

The Gingerbread Man Centers

Math Center

Math Standard
Measures length using nonstandard materials

Measuring with Gingerbread Babies

Materials

- rulers
- tape
- activity master/patterns on page 37
- scissors
- pencil
- crayons or markers

Teacher Preparation: Duplicate the activity master/pattern and cut it in two. Provide each child with a copy of each. Place a book, a pencil, a crayon, and a pair of scissors to be measured in the center.

Have children cut out the two strips of gingerbread babies. Tell children to tape both strips to a ruler. Then have children measure each object in the center with the ruler and count how many gingerbread babies long the object is. Tell children to write the number next to the correct picture on the activity master.

Tip: Many hardware stores will donate wooden rulers that are flat on both sides and work well for this activity.

Reading Center

Language Arts Standard
Sequences events accurately

Sequencing the Story

Materials

- picture cards on page 36
- pocket chart or flannel board
- crayons or markers
- construction paper
- small squares of felt
- scissors
- glue

Teacher Preparation: Duplicate the picture cards, cut them out, and mount them on construction paper. Glue a small square of felt on the back of each card for flannel board use. Display a copy of *The Gingerbread Man* by Eric A. Kimmel or Karen Schmidt in the center.

Read *The Gingerbread Man* to children. Discuss with children the sequence of events in the story. Have children retell the story using the picture sequencing cards.

The Gingerbread Man Centers

Language Center

Language Arts Standard
Recognizes uppercase and lowercase letters

Find the Gingerbread House

Materials

- patterns on page 38
- library pocket
- crayons or markers
- file folders
- scissors
- glue

Teacher Preparation: Make eight copies of the gingerbread house and the gingerbread man. Color them and cut them out. Glue the houses to the inside of two file folders. Glue the library pocket on the outside of the file folder to hold the gingerbread men. Write a capital letter on the round window of each house and a lowercase letter on the tummy of each gingerbread man.

Have children put the gingerbread men on the houses that have matching partner letters.

Sensory Center

Math Standard
Sorts by size and shape

Ginger Dough

Materials

- 2 cups flour
- 2 Tbsp. cream of tartar
- wooden spoon
- rolling pins
- 2–3 drops brown food coloring
- gingerbread man cookie cutters (different sizes and shapes)
- 1 cup salt
- 1 Tbsp. oil
- wax paper
- metal cookie sheet
- 2 cups water
- saucepan
- plastic bag
- ground ginger

Teacher Preparation: Mix the ingredients in a saucepan. Cook over medium heat, stirring until the mixture is stiff. Place it on wax paper to cool and then knead until smooth. Store in an airtight plastic bag.

Have children flatten the play dough with a rolling pin. Invite them to cut out several gingerbread men with the cookie cutters and place them on the cookie sheet. Have them describe the relative sizes.

The Gingerbread Man Centers

Writing Center

Language Arts Standard
Makes illustrations to match stories

Making a Class Book

Materials

- activity master on page 39
- construction paper
- pencil
- hole punch
- crayons
- 1-inch binder rings

Teacher Preparation: Duplicate a copy of the activity master for each child.

Read a traditional version of *The Gingerbread Man* to children. Have children write or dictate the name of a different animal that the gingerbread man might run away from. Encourage children to draw a picture of the animal.

Make a cover using construction paper and bind the pages to make a class book.

Game Center

Social Studies Standard
Follows rules such as taking turns

Run, Run as Fast as You Can

Materials

- none

Have children sit in a circle. Choose one child to be the gingerbread man. Have the child walk around the circle slowly chanting, "Run, run, as fast as you can. You can't catch me, I'm the gingerbread man." When the "gingerbread man" gets to the word *man*, he or she touches a seated child on the head and runs around the circle to the nearest empty spot. The seated child gets up and chases the "gingerbread man" and tries to catch him or her. If the "gingerbread man" is caught before reaching the empty seat, he or she sits in the middle of the circle the next round. The child who did the chasing is now the "gingerbread man." If the "gingerbread man" is not caught, he or she walks around the circle chanting again and the chasing child returns to his or her seat.

Puppet Pieces Patterns

Use with "Gingerbread Man Puppet" on page 26.

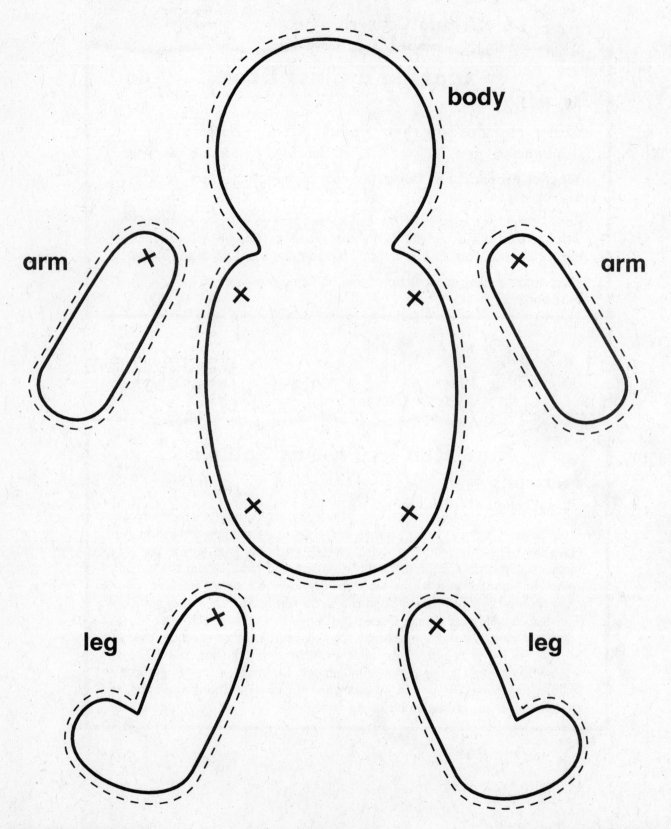

body

arm

arm

leg

leg

Gingerbread Man Pattern

Use with "Stuffed Gingerbread Man" on page 26 and "Gingerbread Cookies" on page 29.

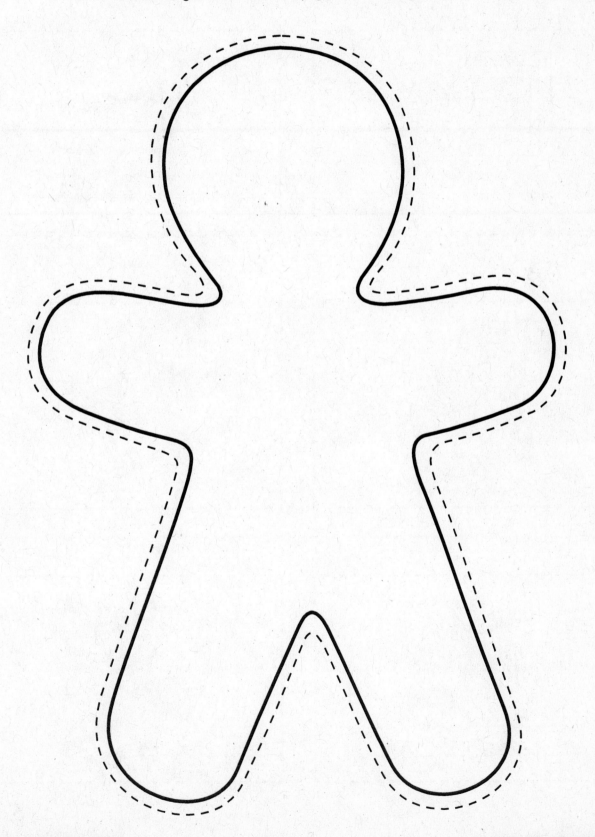

Three Cheers for January PreK–K, SV 9312-2

Picture Sequencing Cards

Use with "Sequencing the Story" on page 31.

Three Cheers for January PreK–K, SV 9312-2

Name _____

Gingerbread Babies

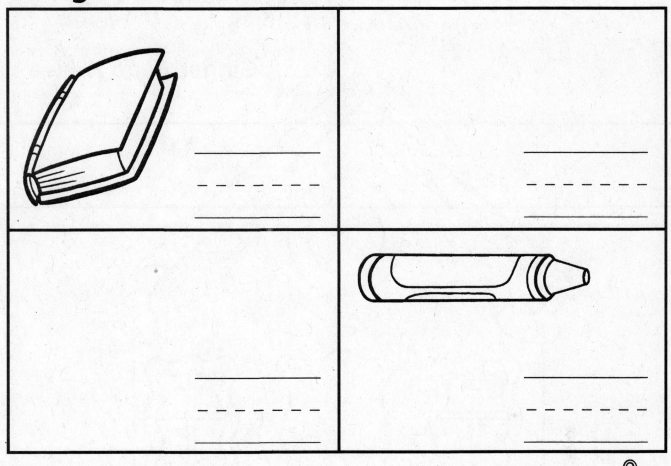

Directions: Use with "Measuring with Gingerbread Babies" on page 31. Have children cut out the two strips of the gingerbread babies. Tell children to tape both strips to a ruler. Then have children measure each object in the center with the ruler and count how many gingerbread babies long the object is. Tell children to write the number next to each picture.

Three Cheers for January PreK–K, SV 9312-2

Gingerbread House and Gingerbread Man Patterns

Use with "Find the Gingerbread House" on page 32.

Gingerbread House

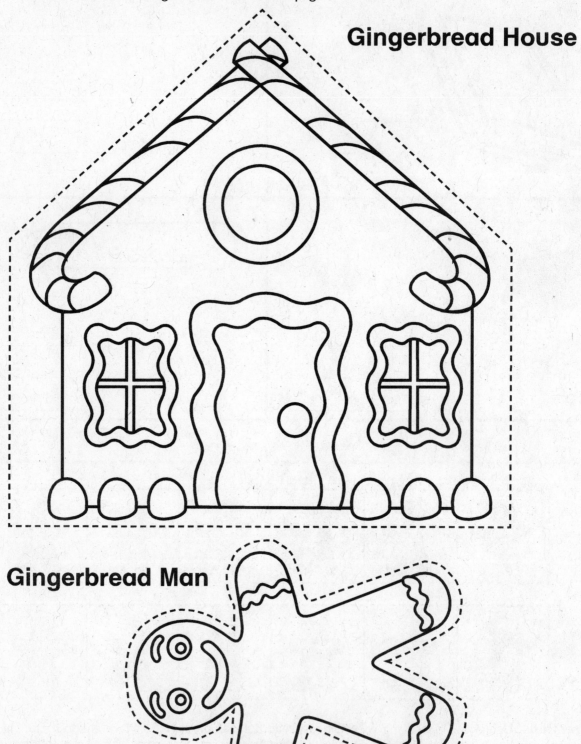

Gingerbread Man

Name _____

Class Book

He ran from a _____.

Directions: Use with "Making a Class Book" on page 33. Have children write or dictate the name of a different animal that the gingerbread man might run away from. Encourage children to draw a picture of the animal.

Three Cheers for January PreK–K, SV 9312-2

Winter Fun

What Happens in Winter

 The winter season begins on December 21 and ends on March 20.

 Snow can form in any cloud that is layered. However, the water droplets in the clouds can freeze if the temperature is too cold. This prevents snowflakes from forming.

 Snowflakes start as tiny ice crystals. When the crystals fall, they attach to other crystals to form a snowflake. Snowflakes usually have six sides.

 As they fall from the clouds, snowflakes pick up pollution that is in the air. Even though snow looks clean enough to eat, it contains pollutants from the environment.

 The food sources of some animals, such as bears, disappear during the winter. These animals hibernate through the winter months.

 Other animals, such as birds, migrate to a warmer climate during the winter months.

 Many animals adapt to winter weather by growing an extra layer of fur or feathers.

 Some animals also turn a different color in the winter to protect themselves from predators.

Three Cheers for January PreK–K, SV 9312-2

Puffy Snowman

Materials

- patterns on page 49
- 6-inch paper plates
- 8-inch paper plates
- assorted buttons
- black beans
- orange and black construction paper
- fabric
- pompoms
- stapler
- glue
- tape
- shaving cream
- scissors

Directions

Teacher Preparation: Provide a black hat and an orange nose pattern for each child. Cut out and form a cone-shaped nose. Use tape to hold it together. Staple together a small and a large paper plate for the body and head of the snowman. Make a hole in the smaller plate where the nose will go. Cut 2" by 18" fabric strips. Make a mixture with an equal amount of glue and shaving cream.

1. Use hands to cover the paper plates with the glue and shaving cream mixture.
2. Glue two buttons for eyes, black beans for mouth, and 2 or 3 pompoms for buttons.
3. Cut out and glue on the hat.
4. Tie a fabric strip around the snowman for a scarf.
5. Push the orange cone through the hole for a nose.

Note to Teacher: Both of these crafts use a shaving cream and glue mixture that has a puffy texture when dried.

Marshmallow Igloos

Materials

- 6-inch paper plates
- 6-oz. styrofoam cups
- mini-marshmallows
- shaving cream
- glue
- small construction paper triangles
- toothpicks
- black marking pen
- regular marshmallows cut in half

Directions

Teacher Preparation: Cut one inch off the top of the cup and glue the cup facedown to the center of the paper plate. Glue a marshmallow half next to the cup to form the igloo's doorway. Make a mixture with an equal amount of glue and shaving cream. Write child's name on a paper triangle and glue it to a toothpick for a flag.

1. Spread glue over all sides of the cup.
2. Stick mini-marshmallows on all sides of the cup.
3. Use hands to spread shaving cream and glue mixture to cover marshmallows.
4. Stick the flag in a marshmallow on the top of the igloo.

Silly Snowmen

You will need

- round cookies
- white frosting
- chocolate chips
- candy corn
- raisins
- red licorice
- pretzel sticks
- craft sticks

Directions

1. Use craft sticks to spread frosting on two cookies for the snowman shape.

2. Add chocolate chips for the eyes, a candy corn for the nose, and a piece of licorice for the mouth.

3. Add raisins for the buttons.

4. Stick pretzels on for the arms using a dab of frosting.

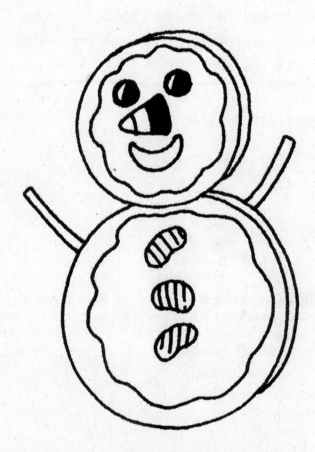

Three Cheers for January PreK–K, SV 9312-2

Five Silly Snowmen

(Sing to the tune of "Muffin Man.")

Duplicate the pattern on page 50 to make five hats and attach each one to a sentence strip.
Have children role-play the snowmen and pretend to melt.

Five silly snowmen—they were fat, they were fat, they were fat.

Five silly snowmen—they were fat and each wore a funny hat.

Out came the sun and melted one, melted one, melted one.

Out came the sun and melted one—oh, how sad was that?

Four silly snowmen—they were fat, they were fat, they were fat.

Four silly snowmen—they were fat and each wore a funny hat.

Out came the sun and melted one, melted one, melted one.

Out came the sun and melted one—oh, how sad was that?

Repeat using the numbers three, two, and one.

Warm Up to These Winter Stories

Geraldine's Big Snow by Holly Keller (Morrow, William and Company)

Millions of Snowflakes by Mary McKenna Siddals (Houghton Mifflin Company)

The Hat by Jan Brett (Puffin Publishing Group)

The Jacket I Wear in the Snow by Shirley Neitzel (Morrow, William and Company)

The Mitten by Jan Brett (Puffin Publishing Group)

Sadie and the Snowman by Allen Morgan (Scholastic)

Three Cheers for January PreK–K, SV 9312-2

Snowflakes Are Special

Materials

- pattern on page 51
- blue construction paper
- blue craft paper
- mini-marshmallows
- glue
- scissors
- iridescent glitter
- small paintbrush
- stapler

Directions

Teacher Preparation: Staple blue craft paper to the bulletin board. Duplicate the pattern to provide a snowflake for each child. Cut out the snowflakes and glue them to blue construction paper for reinforcement.

1. Glue marshmallows on the snowflake.

2. Brush marshmallows with a light coat of glue.

3. Sprinkle iridescent glitter on the snowflake.

Staple the snowflakes on the bulletin board in a pleasing arrangement. Add a coordinating border and the title.

Three Cheers for January PreK–K, SV 9312-2

Winter Centers

Sensory Center

Science Standard
Understands properties of objects

Snow and Ice

Materials

- 5-lb. bag of flour
- measuring cups
- plastic tub
- sifter
- clear, smooth stones
- slotted spoons

Teacher Preparation: Fill the sensory tub with flour and stones. The clear smooth stones can be purchased from the florist department of any garden center.

Have children use the spoons to find the "ice" stones that are hidden in the "snow."

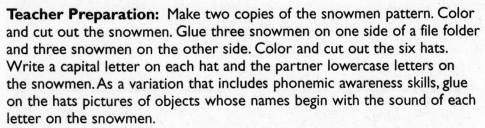

Language Center

Language Arts Standard
Recognizes uppercase and lowercase letters

Where's My Hat?

Materials

- patterns on page 52
- crayons or markers
- file folder
- scissors
- glue

Teacher Preparation: Make two copies of the snowmen pattern. Color and cut out the snowmen. Glue three snowmen on one side of a file folder and three snowmen on the other side. Color and cut out the six hats. Write a capital letter on each hat and the partner lowercase letters on the snowmen. As a variation that includes phonemic awareness skills, glue on the hats pictures of objects whose names begin with the sound of each letter on the snowmen.

Have children put the hats on the snowmen, matching the partner letters or beginning sounds.

Winter Centers

Writing Center

Language Arts Standard
Writes sentences and uses ending punctuation

Snow Sentences

Materials

- paper
- crayons or markers
- pencils
- sentence strips

Have children complete the sentence: I can _____ in the snow. Write each child's response on a sentence strip. Then have each child copy his or her sentence on a piece of paper. Encourage children to draw a picture to illustrate their sentence.

Art Center

Science Standard
Understands properties of materials

Frozen Art

Materials

- ice cube trays
- water
- food coloring
- craft sticks
- white drawing paper

Teacher Preparation: Fill ice cube trays with water and add a few drops of food coloring to each cube. Add a craft stick to each cube and freeze.

Have children hold a craft stick to rub frozen colored ice cubes across white paper. Beautiful colors will appear as the ice melts and different colors blend.

Winter Centers

Math Standard
Associates numerals up to 10 with sets of objects

Math Center

Hot Chocolate Math

Materials

- pattern on page 53
- small container
- construction paper
- mini-marshmallows
- crayons
- glue

Teacher Preparation: Duplicate the pattern to make 10 copies. Color, cut out, and glue the mugs to construction paper to make 10 counting mats. Write a number from 1 to 10 on each mat. Place marshmallows in a small container.

Have the children spread the counting mats on the table or floor. Challenge them to count the corresponding number of marshmallows to match the number on each mat. The mats may also be used for math storyboards.

Tip: Have extra marshmallows for children to eat after they have finished the activity.

Math Standard
Associates numerals up to 10 with sets of objects

Game Center

Snowball Bowling

Materials

- 5 or 6 two-liter soda bottles
- polyester fiberfill
- scissors
- white spray paint
- needle and thread
- markers
- old sock

Teacher Preparation: Spray soda bottles with white paint. Draw a snowman outline and features on the side of each bottle. Cut off the foot of the sock and stuff it with fiberfill until it has a ball shape. Stitch the sock closed with needle and thread.

Have children stand the snowmen soda bottles in a row. Invite children to stand several feet away and try to knock the bottles down by tossing the "snowball" at them. Have them count the number of bottles they knock down.

Winter Centers

Reading Center

The Hat: A Flannel Board Story

Materials

- flannel board
- felt
- patterns on pages 54 and 55
- glue
- scissors

Teacher Preparation: Duplicate the patterns and cut them out. Glue a small square of felt to the back of each one.

Read *The Hat* by Jan Brett. Discuss with children the sequence of the story. Invite children to retell the story using the flannel board pieces.

Science Center

Frozen Pennies

Materials

- metal loaf pan
- spoons
- water
- plastic safety goggles
- pennies
- pan scale

Teacher Preparation: Fill a loaf pan with water and partially freeze it. Add pennies and freeze it completely. Allow the frozen block to thaw 30 minutes before using and then remove it from the pan.

Discuss with children how ice melts and turns into water. Have one child put on safety goggles. Then have the child chip away the ice with the spoon to find the pennies. Encourage the child to continue until a designated number of pennies are found.

Caution: For safety reasons, allow only one child at a time to use this center.

Hat and Nose Patterns

Use with "Puffy Snowman" on page 41.

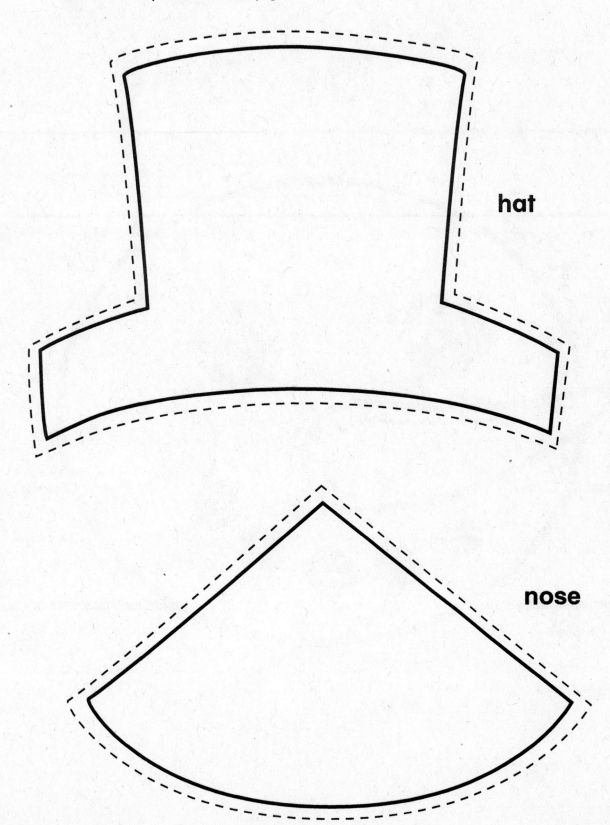

hat

nose

Three Cheers for January PreK–K, SV 9312-2

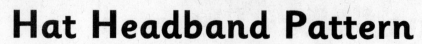

Hat Headband Pattern

Use with "Five Silly Snowmen" on page 43.

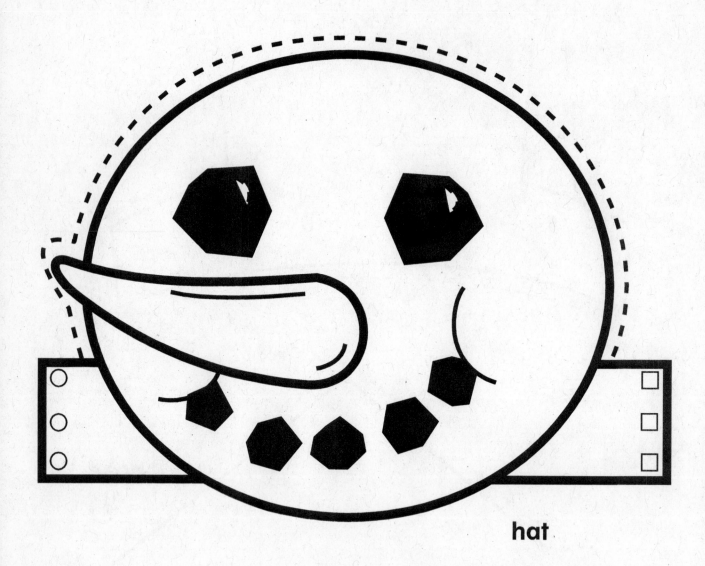

hat

Three Cheers for January PreK–K, SV 9312-2

Bulletin Board Pattern

Use with "Snowflakes Are Special" on page 44.

snowflake

Snowmen and Hats Patterns

Use with "Where's My Hat?" on page 45.

hat

hat

hat

snowman

snowman

snowman

52

Unit 4, Winter: Patterns
Three Cheers for January PreK–K, SV 9312-2

Mug Counting Boards Pattern

Use with "Hot Chocolate Math" on page 47.

Girl and Clothing Patterns

Use with "*The Hat:* A Flannel Board Story" on page 48.

Three Cheers for January PreK–K, SV 9312-2

Animal Patterns

Use with "*The Hat:* A Flannel Board Story" on page 48.

Three Cheers for January PreK–K, SV 9312-2

Penguins

Penguins are one of the few kinds of birds that cannot fly. There are 17 species of penguins that live in the Southern Hemisphere. The larger species live in the coldest areas.

Penguins are excellent swimmers and can stay underwater for several minutes at a time.

They are warm-blooded animals that are covered with a layer of fat, a layer of down feathers, and a layer of feathers. Penguins rub oil from a gland to help waterproof their feathers.

Their main diet is fish, but they will eat squid, octopus, and shrimp.

Penguins drink saltwater from the ocean. They have a special gland in their bodies that removes the salt from the water and pushes it out of the grooves in their bill.

During the mating season, penguins head for a special nesting area on the shore called a rookery. A penguin stays with its mate as long as they have chicks.

The Adélie penguin is the most common species in Antarctica. It builds its nest with rocks.

Depending on the species, the female lays one or two eggs at a time. The emperor penguin lays only one egg at a time.

The male emperor penguin cares for the egg while the female leaves in search of food. The male stands with the egg on his feet under a brood pouch for up to nine weeks. He lives off of stored fat in his body.

Once the chick hatches and is strong enough, both the male and the female leave in search of food. The chick is left in a group with other chicks. The parents recognize their chick by the sound it makes.

Three Cheers for January PreK–K, SV 9312-2

Footprint Penguin

Materials

- 6" x 9" black construction paper
- orange construction paper
- white tempera paint
- paintbrushes
- chalk
- wiggly eyes
- scissors
- glue

Directions

Teacher Preparation: Trace the shape of the child's shoe with chalk on black paper.

1. Cut out the shoe shape.
2. Paint a white oval on the large end of the shoe shape for the penguin's tummy.
3. Glue on two wiggly eyes.
4. Draw a small triangle on orange paper for the penguin's beak.
5. Cut out the beak and glue it below the eyes.
6. Draw two penguin feet on orange paper.
7. Cut out the feet and glue them on the penguin's body.

Tip: Younger children may need help drawing the beak and feet shapes.

Penguin Mask

Materials

- patterns on page 65
- 9-inch paper plates
- paintbrushes
- scissors
- hole punch
- stapler
- elastic cord
- black pony beads
- black feathers
- tape
- black and orange tempera paint

Directions

Teacher Preparation: Cut out the patterns to use as a template. Trace the template on a paper plate. Cut out the mask, the eye holes, and the beak. Staple the beak to the nose section of the mask.

1. Paint the beak orange.
2. Paint the mask black.
3. Tape a few feathers to the top of the mask.
4. Punch a hole on each side of the mask.
5. Thread each end of the elastic cord through a punched hole in the mask and through one bead. Tie a knot to secure.

Tip: The bead will prevent the elastic from tearing the paper plate when the child puts on the mask.

Cookie Penguins

You will need

- chocolate cookies with a white cream filling (2 per child)
- small orange jellybeans
- chocolate chips
- white frosting in a tube
- paper plates

Directions

Teacher Preparation: Twist off one side of the cookie and break it into two equal parts.

1. Lay the cookie on a plate with the white cream side showing for penguin body.

2. Place broken cookie halves next to the body for the wings.

3. Place the second cookie on the plate for the head.

4. Use a small amount of frosting to attach two chocolate chips for the eyes and an orange jellybean for the beak.

5. Use a small amount of frosting to attach two jellybeans for the feet.

Three Cheers for January PreK–K, SV 9312-2

♫ Penguin Family

(Sing to the tune of "Itsy Bitsy Spider.")

The little mother penguin waddled on two legs.

She went to her nest and laid a round egg.

Then she was hungry and wanted to eat.

So the daddy penguin rolled the egg up on his feet.

He kept the egg warm till the mommy came back.

While he took his turn to eat, the egg began to crack.

Out came a baby chick, fuzzy and gray,

Which made the penguins happy on that special day.

Perfect Penguin Books

Antarctic
by Helen Cowcher (Sunburst)

Cinderella Penguin
by Janet Perlman (Puffin)

Little Penguin's Tale
by Audrey Woods (Voyager Books)

Penguin Pete
by Marcus Pfister (North South Books)

Tacky the Penguin
by Helen Lester (Houghton Mifflin)

The Emperor's Egg
by Martin Jenkins (Candlewick Press)

The Penguin Family Book
by Lauritz Somme (North South Books)

Penguins Play

Materials

- pattern on page 66
- blue and white craft paper
- black and orange construction paper
- scissors
- glue
- white chalk
- paintbrushes
- white and orange tempera paint

Directions

Teacher Preparation: Cover the bulletin board with blue and white craft paper to resemble an ice slope and sky. Trace the penguin body and wing patterns on black construction paper. Trace the foot pattern on orange construction paper. Provide patterns for each child.

Discuss with children that penguins love to play. They make a line and take turns sliding on their tummies down the slope. After a turn, they go back to the end of the line to wait for another turn.

1. Cut out the penguin body and wing. Glue the wing on the body.

2. Paint a white tummy on the body and paint the beak orange.

3. Draw an eye with white chalk.

4. Cut out the orange foot and glue on the body.

Arrange some penguins standing in a line on the ice cliff, some sliding down the hill on their tummies, and some walking to the back of the line. Add a border.

Three Cheers for January PreK–K, SV 9312-2

Penguins Centers

Block Center

Math Standard
Uses familiar manipulatives to recognize shapes and their relationships

Penguins on Ice

Materials

- black tempera paint
- large piece of blue felt
- orange and white craft foam
- hot glue gun
- scissors
- glue
- clean 7-ounce plastic cups or containers that have a penguin shape

Teacher Preparation: Use the materials to make penguins. Paint the containers black except for an oval for the penguin's tummy. Cut out two small circles from the white craft foam for the eyes. Draw black part of the eye with a marker. Cut out a small triangle from the orange craft foam for the beak. Glue eyes and beak on each container. Lay a large piece of felt on the floor for the ocean.

Have children use blocks to build an "ice cliff" that the penguins can climb on. Tell children to build a ramp from the "ice cliff" to the ocean. Then have children take turns helping penguins climb to the top of the cliff and slide into the water.

Language Center

Language Arts Standard
Recognizes uppercase and lowercase letters

Penguin Partners

Materials

- activity master on page 67
- pencil
- crayons

Teacher Preparation: Duplicate the activity master and write a capital letter and a matching lowercase letter on pairs of penguins. Write a capital letter and a lowercase letter that does not match on other pairs. Provide a copy of the activity master for each child.

Have children use a pencil to trace the letters. Then have children color each pair of penguins that have partner letters.

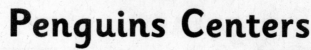

Penguins Centers

Writing Center

Language Arts Standard
Writes words that move left to right

Snow Writing

Materials

- black construction paper
- white tempera paint
- sentence strips
- masking tape
- black markers
- quart-size plastic bag

Teacher Preparation: Tape construction paper to the table. Fill the plastic bag with a small amount of white tempera paint. Remove as much air as possible before sealing the bag. The paint should cover the entire bag when sealed flat. Write *PENGUIN*, *EGG*, *CHICK*, or *FEATHERS* on sentence strips.

Have children lay the plastic bag flat on the black construction paper. Have them select a word card. Invite children to use one finger to write the first letter of the word on the top of the plastic bag. Children may use the palm of their hand to erase. Have them repeat the procedure until the remaining letters of the word are written.

Art Center

Science Standard
Understands the characteristics of organisms

Thumbprint Penguins

Materials

- 4½" x 9" light blue construction paper
- white and orange tempera paint
- toothpicks
- black ink pad
- pencil with unused eraser
- fine-tip black marker

Have children press their index finger on the ink pad and print several fingerprints on the blue paper. Then invite the children to dip the eraser end of a pencil in white paint and press it in the middle of each fingerprint for the penguin's tummy. Next, have children use the marker to add two black dots on each fingerprint for penguin eyes. Then have children dip the end of a toothpick in orange paint and make a tiny dot for the penguin beak and two dots for the feet.

Penguins Centers

Math Center

Math Standard
Connects number words and numerals to the quantities they represent

Count the Steps Board Game

Materials

- file folder
- die or spinner
- scissors
- crayons or markers
- two different colored plastic chips
- patterns on pages 68 and 69
- glue

Teacher Preparation: Duplicate the board game patterns. Cut them out and glue them onto a file folder. Color the penguins. Cut them out and glue the adult penguins on the starting space and the chick on the ending space.

Discuss with children that the mother and father penguins recognize their chick by the sound it makes. Have children play the game to see if the mother or father finds the chick first. Invite each player to select a plastic chip for a marker and take turns rolling the die to determine the number of spaces to move the marker.

Science Center

Science Standard
Understands properties of materials and characteristics of organisms

Waxy Feathers

Materials

- black construction paper
- eyedropper
- white crayon
- cup of water

Teacher Preparation: Cut the black construction paper into fourths.

Tell children that penguins have an oil gland from which they extract oil to cover their feathers. Since they spend up to 75% of their time in the water searching for food, they need this oil to waterproof their bodies.

Have children press very hard on the crayon to color half of one side of the construction paper. Then have them fill an eyedropper with water and squeeze drops of water onto each half of the paper. Encourage children to compare the water drops on the waxy half with those on the plain areas of the paper.

Penguins Centers

Game Center

Science Standard
Understands characteristics
of organisms

Carry the Egg Race

Materials

• beanbag   • masking tape

Teacher Preparation: Place a one-foot piece of masking tape on the floor. From the tape, measure a distance of 6' to 10' and place a second one-foot piece of tape on the floor.

Discuss with children how the emperor penguins care for their eggs. The mother leaves the egg in search of food and is gone for several weeks. The father keeps the egg warm by holding it on his feet and covering it with a pouch of skin. He does not eat until the mother returns. Whenever he moves, he continues to carry the egg.

Invite children to work in pairs. Have each child stand on a piece of tape facing each other. Have children take turns slowly walking the beanbag "egg" to his or her partner and placing it on his or her feet.

Reading Center

Language Arts Standard
Distinguishes words in
sentences

Read the Sentence

Materials

• word cards on page 70
• scissors
• flannel board
• small felt squares
• construction paper
• glue
• sentence strips

Teacher Preparation: Duplicate the word cards on construction paper and cut them apart. Write "*Penguins are black and white.*" and "*I like penguins.*" on sentence strips. Glue a small square of felt on the back of each word card and each sentence strip for flannel board use.

Have a child choose a sentence strip and place it on the flannel board. Then have the child place the word cards below the sentence strip, matching the word order. Ask the child to point to each word and read the sentence.

Mask Patterns

Use with "Penguin Mask" on page 57.

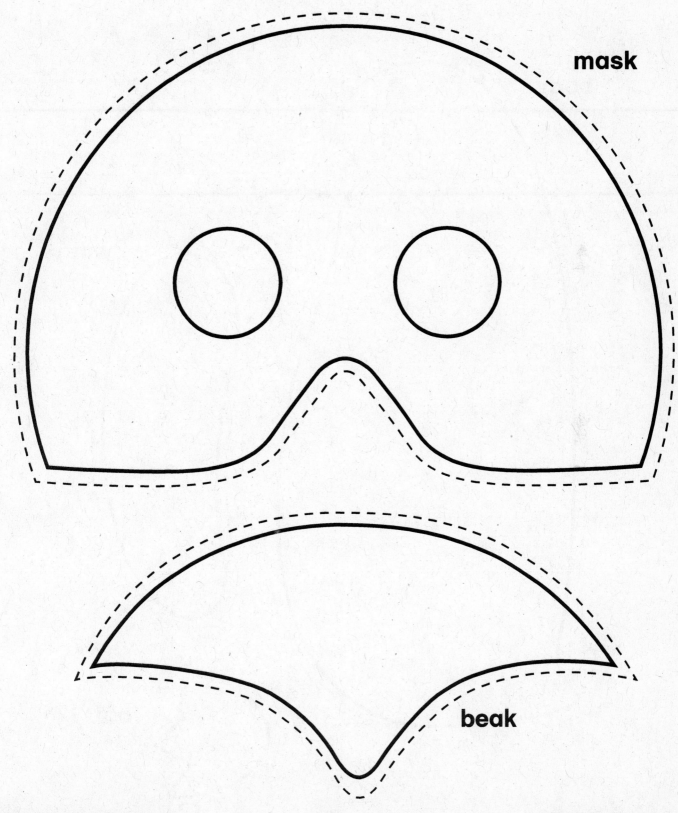

mask

beak

Unit 5, Penguins: Patterns
Three Cheers for January PreK–K, SV 9312-2

Penguin Body, Wing, and Foot Patterns

Use with "Penguins Play" on page 60.

body

wing

foot

Name _____

Partner Letter

Directions: Use with "Penguin Partners" on page 61. Have children use a pencil to trace the letters. Then have children color each pair of penguins that have partner letters.

Unit 5, Penguins: Activity Master
Three Cheers for January PreK–K, SV 9312-2

Board Game Pattern (left side)

Use with "Count the Steps Board Game" on page 63.

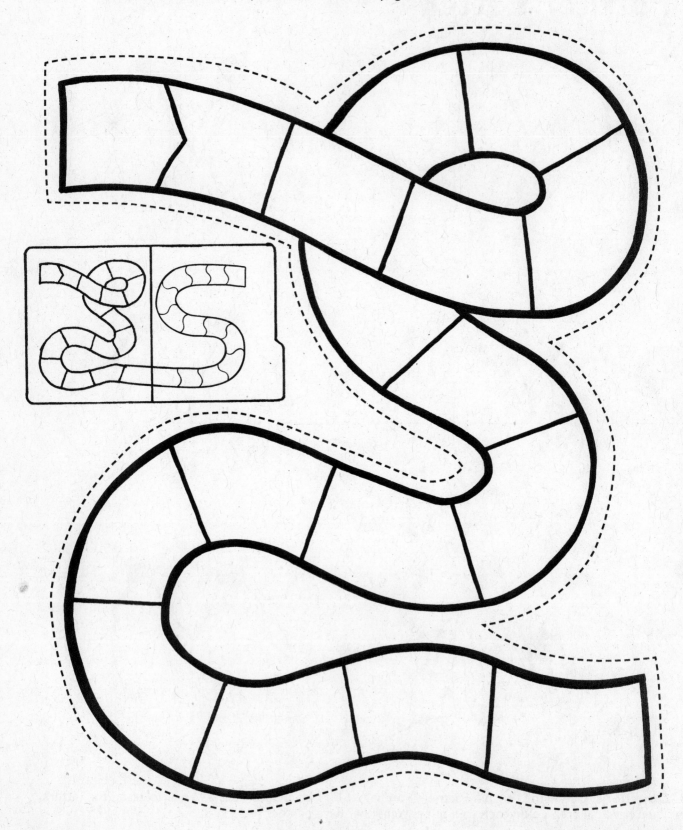

Three Cheers for January PreK–K, SV 9312-2

Board Game Pattern (right side)

Use with "Count the Steps Board Game" on page 63.

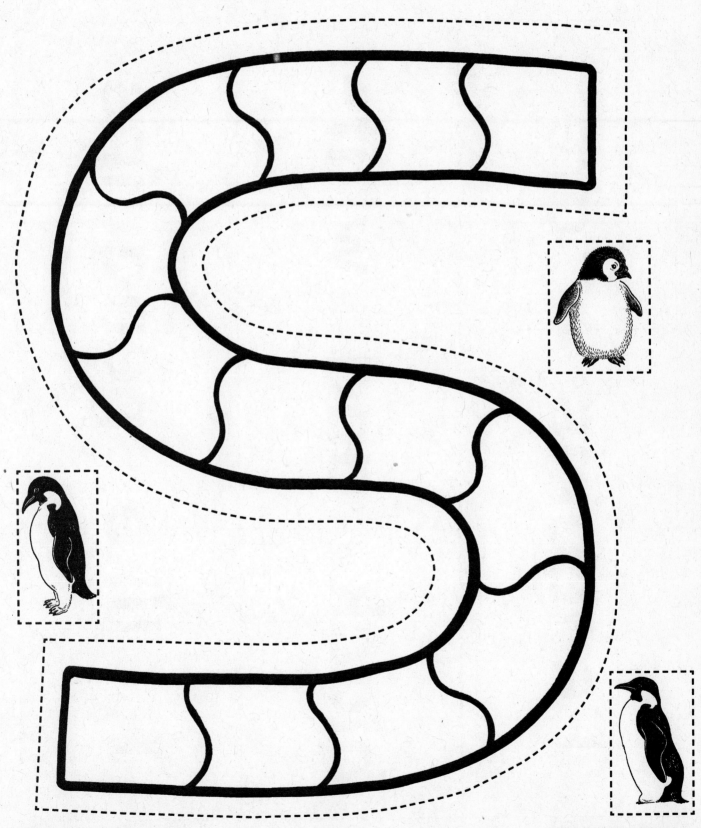

Unit 5, Penguins: Patterns
Three Cheers for January PreK–K, SV 9312-2

Word Cards

Use with "Read the Sentence" on page 64.

are

white.

penguins.

Penguins

and

black

I like

Three Cheers for January PreK–K, SV 9312-2

Dinosaurs

 Dinosaur fossil discoveries have occurred for thousands of years. The fossils were first thought to belong to some type of giant. However, the first person to describe a fossil scientifically was William Buckland. He was a British fossil hunter who discovered Megalosaurus in 1819.

 Over 500 kinds of dinosaurs have been discovered that lived during the Mesozoic Era. This era was divided into three periods: the Triassic, Jurassic, and the Cretaceous.

 Plant-eating sauropods were the largest animals to ever walk the earth, but the blue whale is bigger than a sauropod.

 Most dinosaurs were plant eaters that walked on four legs. Some were meat eaters that walked on two muscular hind legs that provided speed for catching their food.

 The largest dinosaurs were over 100 feet long and up to 50 feet tall. The smallest was the size of a chicken.

 There is no clear evidence that determines whether dinosaurs were warm- or cold-blooded. Some scientists believe that the giant sauropods could have been warm-blooded because of their body size.

 Almost all dinosaurs hatched from eggs. The smallest egg discovered was slightly larger than a turkey egg. The gigantic sauropods laid eggs about the size of a volley ball.

 Scientists do not know for sure how dinosaurs sounded or what color they were.

 Dinosaurs became extinct some 65 million years ago. Some scientists believe that they experienced gradual changes and died out. Others believe that a catastrophic event occurred that caused the extinction of the dinosaurs to happen over a short period of time.

71

Unit 6, Dinosaurs: Teacher Information
Three Cheers for January PreK–K, SV 9312-2

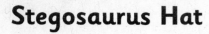

Stegosaurus Hat

Materials

- 4 or 5 paper plates per child
- picture of a stegosaurus
- tempera paints
- paintbrushes
- stapler
- scissors
- hole punch
- yarn

Directions

Display a picture of a stegosaurus and discuss with children the characteristics of the body including the bony plates on the back.

1. Paint the paper plates using desired colors. Allow them to dry.

2. Fold all but one of the plates in half and staple the sides together.

3. Staple the folded plates together end-to-end.

4. Punch a hole on the fold of the plate at the end and tie a short piece of yarn through the hole.

5. Punch a hole on two sides of the remaining paper plate. Tie a 12-inch piece of yarn through each hole.

6. Punch a third hole between the two other holes.

7. Tie the loose end of the yarn that is attached to the folded paper plates through the third hole and tie.

8. Place the flat paper plate on top of the child's head and tie the yarn below the chin so that folded plates hang freely down the child's back.

T. rex Sack Puppet

Materials

- patterns on pages 80 and 81
- brown construction paper
- brown lunch sacks
- scissors
- glue
- 3" x 5" blank index cards
- black crayon or marker

Directions

Teacher Preparation: Duplicate the pattern pieces on brown construction paper. Provide patterns of two arms, two legs, and one tail for each child.

Demonstrate how to turn the sack upside down and glue the arms and legs on the sides of the sack.

1. Cut out two hind legs and glue to sides of sack.

2. Cut out two arms and glue to sides of sack.

3. Fold over the tab on the tail and glue it to the back of the sack.

4. Draw a zigzag line across the length of an index card and cut the card in half along the line.

5. Lift the bottom flap of the sack and glue one zigzag card to the flap for the top teeth. Glue the other zigzag card under the flap for the bottom teeth.

6. Draw fierce looking eyes and nostrils on the bottom of the sack.

7. Write T. rex on the sack.

Three Cheers for January PreK–K, SV 9312-2

Dinosaur Fruit Dig

You will need

- chocolate instant pudding
- milk
- chocolate cookies with a white cream filling
- dinosaur fruit snacks
- 8-oz. clear plastic cups
- spoons
- mixing bowl
- mixer
- measuring cups
- gallon-size plastic bag

Directions

Teacher Preparation: Prepare chocolate pudding according to directions. Crush chocolate cookies in the plastic bag.

1. Fill plastic cup half full with pudding.

2. Stir in one spoonful of crushed cookies.

3. Stir in 5 to 6 dinosaur fruit pieces.

4. Use a spoon to dig out the dinosaurs.

Three Cheers for January PreK–K, SV 9312-2

♫ Dinosaur Friends

(Sing to the tune of "She'll Be Coming 'Round the Mountain.")

Oh, T. rex had very sharp teeth.

Oh, T. rex had very sharp teeth.

He walked on two feet

And ate lots of meat.

Oh, T. rex had very sharp teeth.

Oh, Triceratops had three horns.

Oh, Triceratops had three horns.

He had a frill around his neck

To save him from T. rex.

Oh, Triceratops had three horns.

Oh, Apatosaurus had a long neck.

Oh, Apatosaurus had a long neck.

She ate lots of plants each day

And walked slowly along the way.

Oh, Apatosaurus had a long neck.

Oh, Stegosaurus had plates
on his back.

Oh, Stegosaurus had plates
on his back.

He had a small head

And four spikes on his tail.

Oh, Stegosaurus had plates
on his back.

Daring Dinosaur Books

Big Old Bones
by Carol Carrick (Clarion Books)

**Can I Have a Stegosaurus, Mom?
Can I? Please!?**
by Lois G. Grambling (BridgeWater)

Digging up Dinosaurs
by Aliki (Harper Trophy)

How Do Dinosaurs Get Well Soon?
by Jane Yolen (Blue Sky Press)

How Do Dinosaurs Say Goodnight?
by Jane Yolen (Blue Sky Press)

Patrick's Dinosaurs
by Carrol Carrick (Clarion Press)

Sammy and the Dinosaurs
by Ian Whybrow (Scholastic Inc.)

**The Big Book of Dinosaurs:
A First Book for Young Children**
by Angela Wilkes (DK Publishing)

Unit 6, Dinosaurs: Song and Book List
Three Cheers for January PreK–K, SV 9312-2

Back in Time

Materials

- blue craft paper
- pattern on page 82
- white construction paper
- tempera paints

- sponges
- clothespins
- scissors
- glue

- wiggly eyes
- paintbrushes
- plastic dish or plate for each color of paint

Directions

Teacher Preparation: Enlarge the dinosaur pattern and duplicate it on construction paper. Provide a copy for each child. Cut the sponge into 1-inch squares. Clip each square with a clothespin. Make one sponge for each color of paint. Pour a small amount of each paint into a separate plastic dish.

1. Cut out the dinosaur.

2. Hold onto the clothespin and dip the sponge into paint.

3. Press the sponge onto the dinosaur in a random pattern. Add other colors, if desired.

4. Glue on a wiggly eye.

Have children paint a background mural on the blue craft paper. Have them include trees, mountains, a river, and a volcano. Cover the bulletin board with the mural, and staple the dinosaurs to the background. Add a border and the caption.

Three Cheers for January PreK–K, SV 9312-2

Dinosaur Centers

 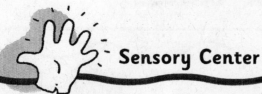

Sensory Center

Science Standard
Understands characteristics of organisms

Dinosaur Dig

Materials

- large plastic tub
- small plastic dinosaurs
- sand
- spoons
- plastic eggs

Teacher Preparation: Fill plastic tub with sand and put plastic dinosaurs inside the eggs. Hide the eggs in the sand.

Discuss with children how dinosaurs hatched from eggs. Then have children dig the eggs out of the sand with a spoon. Ask them to open the eggs to find the dinosaurs. Have children hide the eggs and repeat the activity.

Puzzle Center

Social Studies Standard
Understands the importance of jobs

Dinosaur Puzzle

Materials

- dinosaur puzzle
- plastic tub
- 2 packages of white navy beans

Teacher Preparation: Fill the plastic tub with beans. Mix in the dinosaur puzzle pieces.

Discuss with children how paleontologists dig dinosaur bones from stone and then put them together like a puzzle. Have children find the puzzle pieces in the "rocks." Challenge them to put the pieces together to complete the puzzle.

Dinosaur Centers

Writing Center

Language Arts Standard
Writes messages, labels, or captions

Describing Dinosaurs

Materials

- activity master on page 83
- pencil
- crayons

Teacher Preparation: Provide a copy of the activity master for each child.

Discuss with children what color they think the dinosaurs were. Have children choose a color and draw a picture of a dinosaur. Encourage children to write or dictate a word that describes the size or color of the dinosaur.

Art Center

Science Standard
Understands characteristics of organisms

Pasta Dinosaur

Materials

- black construction paper
- chalk
- pasta of different shapes
- glue

Teacher Preparation: For younger children, draw a simple dinosaur skeleton on the black paper with chalk. Include the skull, vertebrae, ribs, and leg bones.

Have children glue pasta on black paper to form a dinosaur skeleton.

Dinosaur Centers

Math Center

Math Standard
Creates a simple graph

Graph the Dinosaurs

Materials

- activity master on page 84
- 1 to 8 small plastic stegosaurus figures
- 1 to 8 small plastic apatosaurus figures
- 1 to 8 small plastic triceratops figures
- 1 to 8 small plastic pterodactyl figures
- 1 to 8 small plastic tyrannosaurus rex figures
- crayons
- sand
- plastic shoe box
- plastic container

Teacher Preparation: Duplicate a copy of the activity master for each child. Fill the shoe box halfway with sand. Hide the plastic dinosaurs in the sand making sure that there are no more than eight of any one kind. Vary the amounts of each kind of dinosaur.

Demonstrate to children how to color in a section on the graph for each dinosaur that they find. Challenge them to discover which type of dinosaur they find the most of, the least of, and the same number of.

Have children find a dinosaur in the sand and then find that dinosaur on the activity sheet. Have them color one box above the correct dinosaur to represent each dinosaur they find. After they color the box, have them place the dinosaur in the plastic container. Encourage them to repeat the procedure until all the dinosaurs are found.

Block Center

Math Standard
Applies and adapts a variety of appropriate strategies to solve problems

Dinosaur Land

Materials

- large plastic dinosaurs
- blue felt
- plastic trees
- scissors

Teacher Preparation: Cut felt in the shape of a lake. Place the dinosaurs and trees on the blue felt.

Invite children to build a trail for the dinosaurs. They can stack blocks at varying heights to make a maze with blocks. Have children move the dinosaurs through the maze.

Dinosaur Centers

Science Center

Science Standard
Understands about scientific inquiry

Digging Up Dinosaurs

Materials

- 5 cups of sand
- 2 cups of water
- small plastic dinosaurs
- safety goggles
- spoons
- 2 cups of plaster of Paris
- mixing container
- aluminum roasting pan
- old paintbrushes

Teacher Preparation: Mix sand and plaster of Paris. Stir in water until thoroughly mixed. Pour into roasting pan and add small dinosaurs. Let dry overnight.

Read *Digging Up Dinosaurs* by Aliki (Harper Trophy). Discuss how paleontologists dig up fossils. Invite children to put on safety goggles and use a spoon and brush to dig out the dinosaurs. Challenge children to explain how they are like paleontologists in this activity.

Language Center

Language Arts Standard
Recognizes uppercase and lowercase letters

Find the Dinosaur

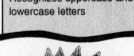

Materials

- activity master on page 85
- crayons

Teacher Preparation: Provide a copy of the activity master for each child.

Have children color the lowercase letters green and the capital letters blue to discover the hidden picture.

T. rex Arms and Legs Patterns

Use with "T. rex Sack Puppet" on page 72.

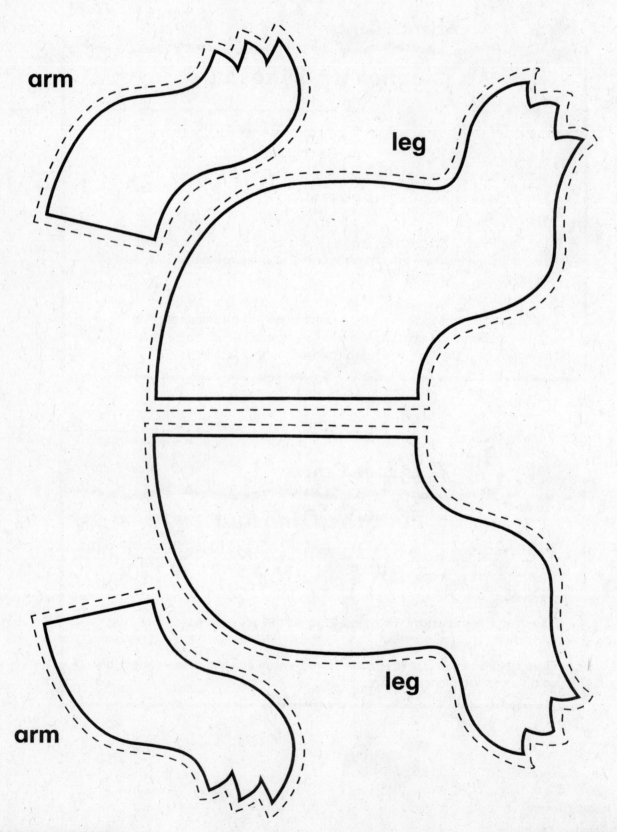

arm

leg

leg

arm

Three Cheers for January PreK–K, SV 9312-2

T. rex Tail Pattern

Use with "T. rex Sack Puppet" on page 72.

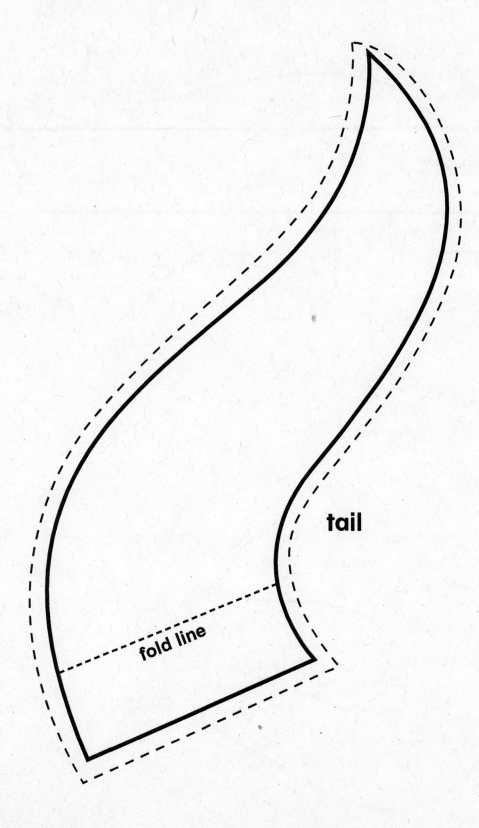

tail

fold line

Three Cheers for January PreK–K, SV 9312-2

Dinosaur Pattern

Use with "Back in Time" on page 75.

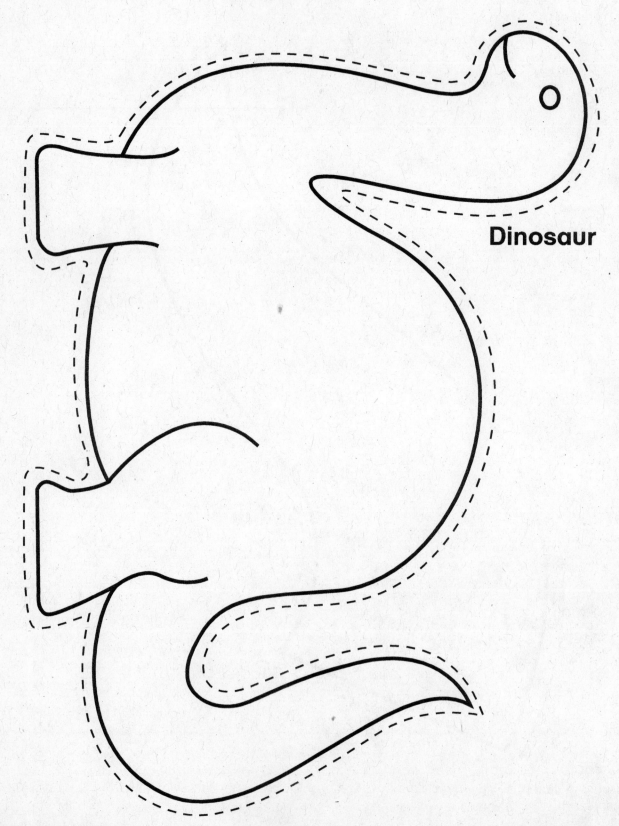

Dinosaur

Three Cheers for January PreK–K, SV 9312-2

Name _____

Describing Dinosaurs

My dinosaur is _____.

Directions: Use with "Describing Dinosaurs" on page 77. Have children choose a color and draw a picture of a dinosaur. Encourage children to write or dictate a word that describes the size or color of the dinosaur.

Unit 6, Dinosaurs: Activity Master
Three Cheers for January PreK–K, SV 9312-2

Name _____

Graph

8				
7				
6				
5				
4				
3				
2				
1				

Directions: Use with "Graph the Dinosaurs" on page 78. Have children find a dinosaur in the sand and then find that dinosaur on the activity sheet. Have them color one box above the correct dinosaur to represent each dinosaur they find.

Unit 6, Dinosaurs: Activity Master
Three Cheers for January PreK–K, SV 9312-2

Dinosaur Puzzle

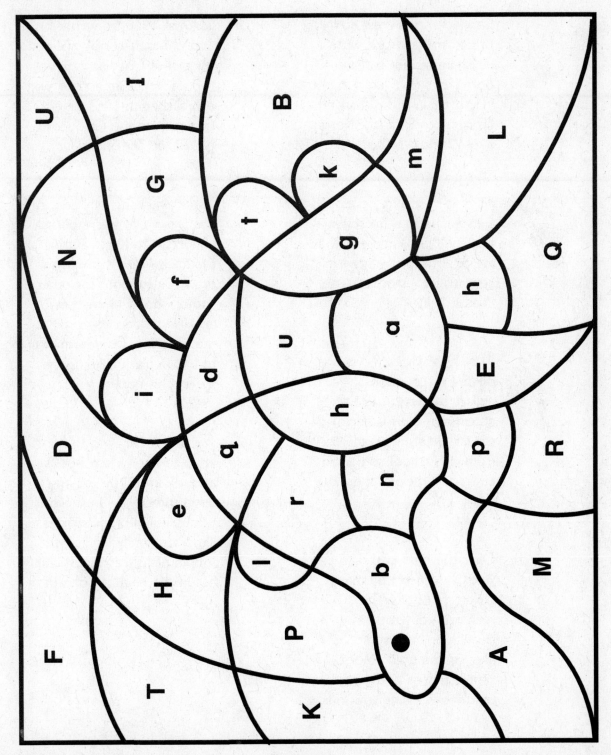

Directions: Use with "Find the Dinosaur" on page 79. Have children color the lowercase letters green and the capital letters blue to discover the hidden picture.

Unit 6, Dinosaurs: Activity Master
Three Cheers for January PreK–K, SV 9312-2

A Look at Ezra Jack Keats

 Ezra Jack Keats grew up in Brooklyn, New York, with Polish immigrant parents. Born Jacob Ezra Jack Katz on March 11, 1916, he changed his name to Ezra Jack Keats after World War II.

 At an early age he developed a strong interest in art. He first sold his paintings at the age of eight for twenty-five cents to local stores to use in advertising.

 After high school, Keats was offered three scholarships to college but was unable to accept them. His father died the day before he graduated from high school, so he had to work to help support the family.

 Over the next several years, he illustrated many children's books. The technique of Keats's illustrations is distinct. He likes to use bold colors, simple shapes, and varied textures in his illustrations.

 Then in 1960, he wrote his first children's book entitled *My Dog Is Lost*. His reputation as an author was established in 1963 when he received the Caldecott Medal for *The Snowy Day*.

 The main character, Peter, in *The Snowy Day* was especially important to Keats. During the many years that he had drawn illustrations for other authors, he had never seen an African-American child as the hero. He was determined to have a black child be the hero in his books.

 The Snowy Day was the first in a series of seven books about a little boy growing up in the city. As in these books, many of his stories illustrate family life and the simple pleasures that a child has in the routines of a day.

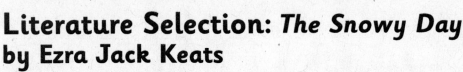

Literature Selection: *The Snowy Day*
by Ezra Jack Keats

Read *The Snowy Day* and have children describe the illustrations in the book. Discuss with them the seasons of the year. Have them imagine what it might be like on the first snowy day of winter. Challenge children to think of different activities they could do in the snow. Then have them complete the following activities about the seasons.

Seasons of the Year
Materials

- activity master on page 90
- scissors
- glue

Directions

Teacher Preparation: Duplicate a copy of the activity master for each child.

Have children cut out the pictures. Ask them to glue each picture in the box next to the season where it belongs.

A Snowy Day
Materials

- pattern on page 91
- bright blue tissue paper
- red tempera paint
- white construction paper
- paintbrush
- scissors
- glue

Directions

Teacher Preparation: Provide a copy of the pattern and a sheet of construction paper for each child. Cut a generous supply of blue tissue paper into 1-inch squares.

Discuss with children that Ezra Jack Keats created his illustrations with different textures and bright colors. Invite children to create a picture of a snowy day.

1. Glue tissue paper squares on the top half of the construction paper to resemble the sky.
2. Leave the bottom half of the paper white for the snow.
3. Cut out the picture of the child.
4. Paint the child's coat red.
5. Glue the picture of the child on the construction paper.

Three Cheers for January PreK–K, SV 9312-2

Books by Ezra Jack Keats

- *A Letter to Amy* (Harper & Row)

- *Apartment 3* (Puffin Books)

- *Dreams* (Viking Books)

- *Goggles* (Macmillan)

- *Hi, Cat!* (Macmillan)

- *Jennie's Hat* (Harper & Row)

- *Louie* (Puffin Books)

- *Peter's Chair* (Harper & Row)

- *Pet Show* (Macmillan)

- *Regards to the Man in the Moon* (Four Winds)

- *The Snowy Day* (Viking Press)

- *The Trip* (HarperCollins)

- *Whistle for Willie* (Viking Books)

For more information visit the website: www.ezra-jack-keats.org

Three Cheers for January PreK–K, SV 9312-2

Bookmark Patterns

A trip to space can be fun in *Regards to the Man in the Moon* by Ezra Jack Keats!

You can "Whistle for Willie" in this story by Ezra Jack Keats!

Pet Show is a blue-ribbon book by Ezra Jack Keats!

Seasons Activity Master

Fall

Winter

Spring

Summer

Directions: Use with "Seasons of the Year" on page 87. Have children cut out the pictures. Ask them to glue each picture in the box next to the season where it belongs.

Child Picture Pattern

Use with "A Snowy Day" on page 87.

Three Cheers for January PreK–K, SV 9312-2

Center Icons

Art Center

Block Center

Dramatic Play Center

Game Center

Center Icons Patterns
Three Cheers for January PreK–K, SV 9312-2

Center Icons

Language Center

Math Center

Music Center

Puzzle Center

Center Icons Patterns
Three Cheers for January PreK–K, SV 9312-2

Center Icons

Reading Center

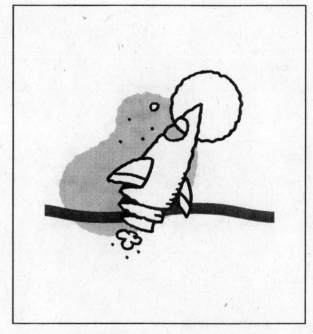

Science Center

Sensory Center

Writing Center

Center Icons Patterns

Three Cheers for January PreK–K, SV 9312-2

Student Awards

Let's celebrate _____'s

Name

progress in _____ .

_____
Teacher's signature

_____
Date

Congratulations, _____ .

You are the January
Student of the Month for

_____

_____
Teacher's signature

_____
Date

Student Awards Patterns
Three Cheers for January PreK–K, SV 9312-2

Student Awards

did

_____

_____

"Dino-saur-ific Work" in _____.

| Teacher's signature | Date |

Calendar Day Pattern

Suggested Uses

- Reproduce one card for each day of the month. Write a numeral on each card and place it on your class calendar. Use cards to mark special days.
- Reproduce to make cards to use in word ladders or word walls.
- Reproduce to make cards and write a letter on each card. Children use the cards to play word games forming words.
- Reproduce to make cards to create matching or concentration games for students to use in activity centers. Choose from the following possible matching skills or create your own:

  uppercase and lowercase letters
  pictures of objects whose names rhyme, have the
      same beginning or ending sounds, or contain
      short or long vowels
  pictures of adult animals and baby animals
  number words and numerals
  colors and shapes
  high-frequency sight words

Student Awards/Calendar Day Pattern
Three Cheers for January PreK–K, SV 9312-2